ACTIVELY CREATIVE

A Guided Process

ACTIVELY CREATIVE

A Guided Process

Victoria Else

USA

Copyright © 2011 by Victoria Else

All Rights Reserved.

ISBN 978-0-9834-0542-9

Photo by Adonai Feria 2011.

Contents

Defining Active Creativity 1
    Intention 3
    Perception 4
    Play 6
Social Barriers to Creativity 9
    Finding Support 10
    Making Corporations More Creative 11
The Active Creative Process 13
    Overview 13
    Preparing for the Process 15
    Step 1: Identification 16
    Step 2: Incubation 16
    Step 3: Insight 18
    Step 4: Evaluation 20
    Step 5: Realization 23
A Quick Guide to Group Brainstorming 25
Exercises and Comments 27
    Creative Process Summary 28
    Exercises for Steps One Through Five 29
    When Do You *Have* to Be Creative? 37
Notes 41
About the Author 43

I. Defining Active Creativity

The topic of this book is active creativity, defined in this book as *the intentional discovery, exploration, and implementation of new solutions to challenges of any type*.

Creativity is not the sole province of geniuses and artists; it is an essential human impulse. Creativity is how your brain explores new experiences and information and integrates them into your understanding of the world. If you were not creative, you would not have been able to adapt to the changing circumstances you have faced in your life; you would still be an infant.

The evidence of creativity is everywhere. Creativity is why we live in houses and eat cooked food, as well as write literature, study the universe, or have industrial revolutions. Every time someone starts a new business or tweaks the knitting pattern for a sweater, they are being creative. Creativity can be used for any purpose, good or bad. (Speaking solely of the process, not the outcome, the development of the atomic bomb was just as creative as the development of penicillin.) What we create is up to us.

Though I'm a poet and I work in the advertising industry, I don't have any special gift for creativity. I'm just someone who is motivated to create. Many of my motivations are simple kinds of problems that occur in everyday life. Because my situation is so ordinary, I believe that if striving for creativity enhances the quality of my life, it could enhance the lives of others as well.

Creativity starts with an inner motivation. It may be stimulated by external inspiration, as when a painter dips a brush into the wrong pot, but finds that the unexpected color brings new life to her work. But what seems to be external stimulus has to find a positive, receptive place inside a human being. When she dipped her brush into the wrong pot, the artist was already yearning for something new. To choose an example from real life, Nobel-winning scientist Ronald Mallett dedicated his brilliant career to understanding the nature of time because of a poignant, impossible wish to go back in time and prevent the early death of his father.

To be fair, there are times when it makes sense to put our minds on automatic, enabling us to multi-task and prioritize. Broadly speaking, though, the alternative to active creativity is passivity; waiting for stimulation, waiting for rescue. That's a lost opportunity. Potential inspiration is everywhere, but we walk right past it on our way to grab our morning cup of coffee. In a passive, routine-locked state we are far more likely to ignore inspiration than we are to take advantage of it. What if more people were looking for inspiration in the world around them? What could we achieve?

Unfortunately, the way our brains work makes mental habits very hard to break. Evolution has shaped us to tease out patterns in the world around us, like which berries are good to eat and how to predict the changing seasons. From one point of view, it could appear that we humans are just creative enough to be good at finding patterns! Yet if we could pull back the camera and look at human history from afar, we would see that there are periods of extraordinary creativity, and, if we pull the camera back far enough, that the entire path of human development has been radically creative.

I believe that the reason for this apparent contradiction between our patterned daily lives and the vast creative scope of human history is that our creative impulse is a reaction how we perceive the world. The single factor that most limits or liberates our creativity is our ability to perceive our environment in an open, receptive way. (In scientific terms, this is called *cognitive flexibility*.) From time to time, large numbers of people seem to take a huge jump together; behind that is usually a new perception of the world, such as the idea that the world is round, not flat. In our individual lives, it may even take loss or tragedy to shake our perceptions and get us to think creatively about our life opportunities.

Is that how things have to be? Of course not. With practice, creativity can become a much bigger part of our normal lives. There are proven techniques to open the windows of our perception and spark creative ideas, even on those bad days when you don't feel like inspiration could possibly strike. In advertising, for example, we are required to be creative every day, and we use specific research and "ideation" techniques to generate new ideas. Other fields such as medicine, scientific research, education, product development, and of course the arts, have their own approaches.

The techniques used by such persistent creators are an important inspiration for this book. But, we should note, by themselves these techniques are insufficient. Many advertisements are repetitive and obvious. Even scientists and artists can be locked into perceptual patterns, using their creativity to tweak things here or there, never breaking through to something truly new. Although this book describes a creative process, it is subordinate to the overall truth that to be creative, *we must find a way to motivate ourselves to push beyond our mental and perceptual habits.*

Overcoming motivational barriers and being creative involves three activities: intention, perception, and play. Each of these topics is explored below.

Intention

Most definitions of creativity derive from the idea of making something new. But in my view newness alone is not sufficient. Newness often arises entirely by accident. When a rock slides from the side of a cliff, it crashes into the earth and forms a new shape. It could even be a beautiful new shape. But was that an act of creation?

Creativity begins with volition, and ends with a plan. It is *intentional*. And intention is a skill as well as a trait. We can train ourselves to form conscious intentions, by thinking about our options, formulating goals, and developing plans. Creative people are notably good at doing this. There's nothing easy about doing something different or doing it in a new way; being creative takes will and drive.

For some reason, people mythologize the notion of accidental creativity. For example, as a child I learned that Alexander Fleming discovered penicillin by "accident." True, he accidentally let mold contaminate a petri dish, where it killed germs he was studying. But his recognition of what the "mold juice" had done and the work he undertook to make good use of that insight were no accidents. On the morning that Alexander Fleming got lucky, he had been searching for ways to kill bacteria and cure diseases for more than ten years. His discovery of penicillin was an intentional act that merely benefited from a stroke of luck.

If my examples of creativity seem purely utilitarian, I apologize. An artist who creates a beautiful sculpture or work of music is also undertaking an intentional act, finding a solution to a challenge even if that challenge only exists in his or her own mind. In one letter to his brother, the painter Vincent Van Gogh described with glee a new problem he'd created for himself: painting three-dimensional scenes using different shades of the same color. Those paintings of orchards in Arles, France, are today are some of the most prized in the world. Needless to say, this too is creativity in action.

The creative challenges we face can also be entirely personal to us, from personal relationships to managing our moods. Finding a solution to an inner conflict certainly requires the intention to create, possibly new thought patterns or different behavior. I also believe when relationships are created intentionally they are much richer and more successful.

As you can see, I don't hold with mystical ideas about creation, at least as pertains to human beings. We are but flesh. Nothing "just happens" because we want it to. Our power to create involves hard, joyous work. In creating, we expose a wishful imagination to the sometimes unforgiving reality of the world. Achieving a creative task requires us to build a strong self that is willing to be tested. What could be more worthwhile?

Perception

Perception as we are using it here means conscious awareness or understanding of input from our senses. In this sense, each of us perceives only a tiny fraction of what exists. Our ability to perceive is limited not only by our sensory limits but also by habitual thoughts and reactions. Finding our daily patterns more convenient and efficient, we rarely test our knowledge or seek out new experiences that might challenge us. As a result, much of what we think we know, we only assume to be true.

In my opinion the trait that most clearly distinguishes actively creative people from others is their willingness to embrace the discomfort of *not* knowing. They disrupt comfortable notions of the world by seeking out new environments, or by trying to perceive familiar things in new ways. Only by doing that can anyone broaden their perceptions.

Take Renaissance man Leonardo da Vinci, one of the greatest artists and inventors of all time. How many of us have sat by a stream and listened to the sound of the water? Relaxing, right? Well, instead of relaxing, da Vinci put his mind and his senses to work. He observed the water and became curious about why it formed specific shapes when it flowed around rocks. He filled pages of his notebook with his drawings and questions.

Da Vinci's famous studies of water flow were, initially, stimulated by simple curiosity that began when he opened his mind and observed his environment. But when he immersed himself in the way water flows, he didn't just passively take it all in. He truly perceived the water, making comparisons and asking new questions, which led him to some of his most profound discoveries.

Eventually, he became curious about how his new perceptions of water could also change his perceptions of other aspects of the world: cognitive flexibility in action. As a result, he engaged in yet more studies and developed still more, related perceptions, leading him to create ideas for engines and mills, and develop an understanding about how blood flows through the body.

Everywhere we go the world offers an endlessly generous palette of topics to become curious about. When you actively reach out into your world to observe it, curiosity naturally flows. If you're willing to really focus, like da Vinci did, your ability to truly perceive your world can become astonishingly rich. By contrast, if you walk the same path over and over again, with your mental habits blinding you, you will never perceive your opportunities to get out and experience anything new.

Right now, someone's next life journey or business breakthrough is hidden by mental habits, within overlooked details and humdrum routine that mask what is truly possible. If you want to shake loose and find a worthy challenge that motivates you to be creative, you need to develop three traits:

- Actively *observe*. Clear away your assumptions and see your world with fresh eyes.

- Be *curious*. Why are things they the way they are? Do they have to be that way? How would you want them to be different?

- *Perceive*. Strive to internalize and understand what you observe, letting what you learn lead you to new ideas.

As you go through your daily routine, work on being observant, curious, and perceptive, and you'll create new muscles for your mind that can make your life richer.

INSPIRATION: CLEARING YOUR MIND

We are rarely truly aware of ourselves or our surroundings. Thoughts are buzzing around in our head, emotions are churning inside of us, and our minds are on anything but what's right under our noses. If we want to perceive and learn from the world around us, we must be consciously focused on it. To do this, you need to clear your mind.

I like to use a simple, ancient meditation exercise to help me prepare for a creative activity. I look at something, for example, the telephone on my desk for a moment, really focusing on its color, shape, anything I can see about it. Then I say to myself, "I am not that [thing]". At that moment, I am thrust back into my own skin, and I suddenly become aware of all of the other things that are going on; the noise of the computer, the sound of traffic outside my window, smells, etc. Now my mind is clear enough to focus on my task.

If this exercise doesn't work for you, look around for other ideas on how to clear your mind. Because this is a problem that faces everyone, there are hundreds of techniques!

Play

Persistent creators—artists, scientific geniuses—are not a different species. They've just engaged their brains in a somewhat different way. Either through training or luck, they have learned to stimulate creative activity in their brains.

For a long time, people thought that creativity was inspired by external spirits like the Muses. Nowadays we are pretty sure that creativity happens right in the human brain. The frontal lobe seems to open the doors to creative ideas and solutions, while the temporal lobe helps you to assess which creative efforts are valuable and insightful. This goes on constantly, day and night, and is essential to our human ability to understand and shape our environment.

Creativity is part of our basic brain function, and in that sense is "always on". That begs the question: why are people ever *un*-creative? As children, we spend much of our time on imaginative play. As adults, the yearning for creativity still exists, though it is often compartmentalized. Possibly, we lighten our daily routines with distracting television shows, passively enjoying other peoples' creativity. But the sense of discovery that we associate with creativity is strangely absent from large portions of our lives.

Scientists have recently discovered why. It's one of those insights that in retrospect seems obvious: creativity requires taking pleasure in what you do; in other words, *playing*, as we did when we were still imaginative children. To be technical about it, creativity thrives on the neurotransmitter dopamine, the brain's reward system. The dopamine system needs our activities to be enjoyable. If you have a creative hobby, you will recognize the pleasure I am talking about, and how different you feel when you are creating than during your typical daily tasks.

To generalize, persistent creators have learned to nurture the enjoyment of creation. In fact, they seek out the dopamine buzz that human beings experience when they are deeply engaged in being creative. My husband is a great example; leave him alone for five minutes and he will start drawing, writing music, or figuring out how to fix something. Of course if we're feeling threatened, for example because we're under scary grownup deadline pressures, or bothered by conflicts, or otherwise just not enjoying life, there's little or no enjoyment. Our need to survive shuts down creativity and tells us to just get things over with.

Please understand that *some* stress is actually good for creativity. Necessity is truly the mother of invention. Sometimes, only strong motivation may drive us to let our brains work out a creative answer. As the original stress blossoms into the deep enjoyment of creation, we may experience a revelation: creativity isn't just a task; it is a beautiful way of life. If that happens, we may permanently redirect our lives onto a more actively creative path.

INSPIRATION: KEEPING PLAY ALIVE

One of the simplest ways to keep your brain in play mode is to smile more often. When you smile, you actually change your emotions and become more optimistic and open-minded.

Try it! The next time you find yourself frowning through your day, sit back, and force a smile. You can try saying or subvocalizing the letter "e"; it helps. Hold it for a while and notice that your body relaxes. Now think about whatever is annoying you, but keep the smile on your face. Take a deep breath. What happens?

When I do this, I sometimes find myself actually laughing. Tension released, I am able to react more positively to problems. This "positive affect" has been shown by researchers to aid in cognitive flexibility, helping me to find solutions that were hidden from my stressed-out self. Others around me also find my smile less intimidating, and are more willing to share ideas. In essence, my smile is inviting them to play with me.

II. Social Barriers to Creativity

The best way to increase our personal creativity is to enjoy challenges instead of dreading them. Yet that's hard to do on our own. Humans are social animals; if others around us are hostile to our creativity, we will probably shut down. By contrast, when people support each other in facing tough problems with optimism instead of fear, creativity happens.

As a teen, I remember becoming so frightened of writing that I stopped for a few years. I couldn't tolerate the sense of distance I experienced when I wrote. I felt that if people around me knew what I was writing, they'd be angry with me. While my experience isn't universal, it exemplifies one force that shuts down creativity: the fear of criticism and rejection. There are individuals who seem immune to this concern. For example, one jazz musician I know of rarely speaks, spending his time almost entirely in making music; social isolation doesn't appear to trouble him. However, he is very unusual. For most of us, of all of the issues we face in being actively creative, our social context is the most important.

When social groups are supportive, creativity can be contagious. My husband, who comes originally from Venezuela, told me of a very poor and remote town which, for no obvious reason, produces talented sculptors. In small huts, surrounded by barefoot children and few belongings, the men carve hauntingly beautiful figures out of a soft local stone, some of which have made it into museums. No-one knows how they started to do this; it's not a widespread cultural pattern. In the next town over, no-one makes sculptures.

More typically, existing social patterns must be overcome for creative new ideas to emerge. A convergence of disparate groups can help, such as occurs in cities. Jazz was born in the port city of New Orleans, among a mix of African Americans, Native Americans, and European sailors and dock workers who wanted to be entertained in local bars. Similarly in Valledupar along the Caribbean coast, slaves fleeing the Spanish blended with local Indian cultures to form a new kind of music called vallenato. Social upheaval can also spark creativity: new ideas central to the American Revolution, such as the right to "pursuit of happiness", took root in the new world largely because the abundance of resources available to all made aristocratic authority obsolete.

Of course, few people in history experience the convergence of different cultures, or live in highly creative communities. Social upheavals don't always produce creative new ideas. Overwhelmingly, the pressure to conform to expectations forms a powerful obstacle to human creativity.

The problem is us. It's easier to make fun of new ideas than it is to understand their potential, especially when they *are* new and not completely formed. The great Gershwin song, "They All Laughed," lists discoverers and inventors who were laughed at before they were proven right. You may want to download the mp3 and listen to it when times get tough—and before you laugh at someone else's new idea.

Finding Support

It seems clear to me that the most important social support we need for creativity is the love and affection of those close to us. Just as when we are children the love of our families makes us feel safe to explore and play, so the love of friends and families can sustain our optimism and willingness to take risks into adulthood. We need that love to overcome our fear of embarrassment, and also to lift our spirits when we fail to achieve a goal.

I'll share one example from my advertising career. A dear friend of mine, a cancer survivor, was given the task of developing a creative idea for a program designed to help people who are undergoing treatment for cancer. Needless to say, this was a very motivating task for her. In addition, the affection that her colleagues felt for her motivated them to get behind her ideas and work harder than usual on bringing them to life in strategy, design, and customer support planning. The result was a breakthrough, award-winning campaign that truly helped people. Yes, even competitive, cynical advertising agencies are filled with real people who are motivated by affection and personal bonds!

That example also shows that access to others with complementary knowledge or expertise is very important to creating anything new. In the end, most creators rely on a social or professional network to supply them with key ingredients for the creative process.

We all need information and expertise we don't already have, as well as positive criticism. You will have to learn for yourself how much input is helpful to you, at what points of your creative process. You will also have to learn who you can and cannot trust to be supportive.

In fact, a supportive environment is so important that I suggest you tap into your own love and concern to find your inspiration. If you are motivated by caring deeply about something beyond yourself, you may find it easier to engage others in the issues that interest you. Your concern can be for your customers, your business partners, your community, the arts, the environment, or of course, your family. Shared concerns create a robust network of support.

Making Corporations More Creative

Many companies try to instill a "culture" of creativity in their organizations. In my experience these efforts tend to fall into two themes: internal competition or inter-group consensus.

First let's examine the impact of a competitive culture. The desire to *surpass* can be a great motivator. Nonetheless, certain types of competition have a particularly negative impact on creativity. Highly competitive people can be domineering, and domination chokes off the free flow of ideas needed for creative convergence.

One of my clients was a successful company which only ten years before had been a tiny start-up. Over time, the company shifted from a nimble innovator to a bureaucratic imitator. What happened? Despite a highly competitive culture, near-worship of the founders put a tight lid on how creative the organization could be. The founders were very domineering people who personally made up or down decisions based on single presentations of an idea.

Believing in competition but unwilling to lose control, they imposed silly bureaucratic processes for groups to compete with one another for funding. Because the processes never worked, they redesigned them every year, absorbing large amounts of management time. But above all, the domineering tone of the leadership discouraged young talent from taking risks. Nobody likes to look foolish, especially a twenty-something just starting out. Told to innovate, employees actually became acolytes to favored corporate stars, hiding in their shadows.

On the other extreme, there are serious downsides to consensus cultures. Though consensus-based companies are much nicer places to work, where people are trained to be respectful and to listen to one another, consensus is not a great way to find creative ideas. The old saying that "too many cooks spoil the soup" is unfortunately quite true. I have worked with many companies that seek diversity of opinion by imposing endless layers of committees and constructing complicated matrix organizations. Despite their good intentions, these confusing webs of responsibility just give too many people the ability to kill ideas—the opposite of what was intended.

There is negative social feedback in consensus organizations as well. Being creative often requires rocking the boat and making other people uncomfortable, but the pressure to be agreeable can drown risk-taking in politically-correct mush. Frankly, the incentives are all wrong.

In the end, I don't buy into the idea that you can establish a "culture" of creativity from the top down. Top-down approaches assume that with the right incentives in place, creativity will just naturally happen. Occasionally this may work; then again, occasionally people are also struck by lightning. No. Creativity is a skill that must be honed; incentives are important, but not sufficient to make people to be creative.

Instead, train managers and workers alike to nurture and sponsor the creative process, right where the work actually gets done. If you do that, the culture will take care of itself. A well-documented example of this approach is the quality circle, in which line workers are given the training, time and resources to develop ideas and fixes to improve products and avoid errors. Where teamwork is needed, the team structure is kept open, drawing on different types of expertise as required. Co-operation is encouraged by acknowledging everyone's contribution. And because decision-making is kept closer to the mid-management level, decision makers have the hands-on expertise needed to get results.

Lastly, if you seek a work situation that will enable you to be creative, don't ask about incentives, ask about support. Be specific. When it comes to which ideas are pursued, who decides? It shouldn't be some distant manager who takes no responsibility for day to day activities. How long does it take for a decision to be made? It shouldn't take forever. And if they use the word "culture", be very, very suspicious.

III. The Active Creative Process

In this chapter, I go through each step of the creative process illustrated below, and give you suggestions for how to start and sustain a creative project. The best way to use this book is to first read through the entire process, and then go back and take each step one at a time, using the exercises provided at the back of the book.

The Active Creative Process: steps flow from bottom to top because each step builds upon the preceding steps.

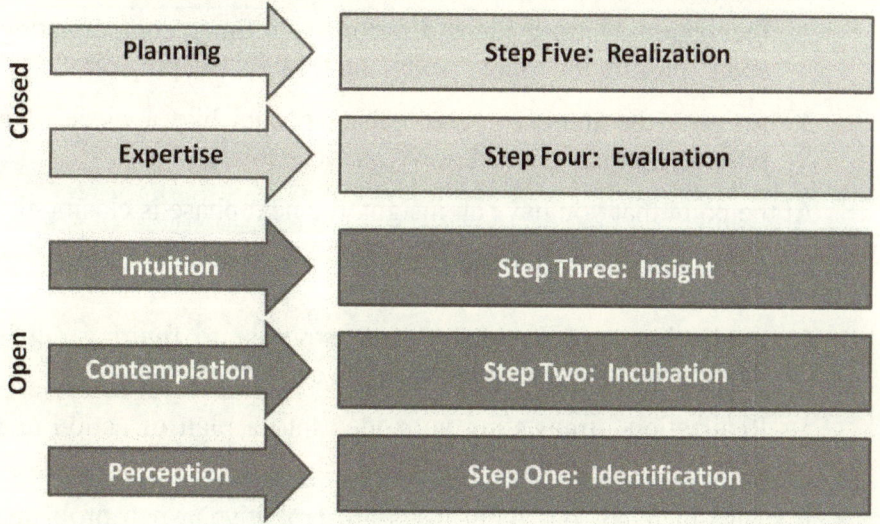

Overview

Have you ever had an idea pop into your head, for example when you woke up after an afternoon nap? That can feel good, but it can also be disorienting when ideas just come out of nowhere, completely out of character for your buttoned-up, hardworking self.

Even our ideas about creativity can make us uncomfortable. For one thing, creativity may *look* weird, with the afflicted person acting spacey, staring at the wall and muttering to themselves, or frowning and typing at a furious pace on their computer. And then you get those stereotypes of tragic geniuses, mad artists and suicidal poets… maybe they make us feel grateful that we're *not* creative.

Does creativity really demand a dangerous surrender to mysterious forces? Luckily, there's always a scientist out there who is ready to demystify things. Some very smart people have dug into what makes creativity happen, and while it's not easy, it's not weird, either.

My favorite author on the subject, Mihaly Csiksentmihalyi (*Creativity,* 1996), described five steps employed by highly creative people. I've reframed them to zero in on making creativity an active, intentional process for everyone.

The process begins with opening the window of creativity:

1. Identification—immersing yourself in a perception that makes you curious; feeling interest until you identify a motivating challenge
2. Incubation—letting ideas develop over time; contemplating and exploring the topic openly and freely; "sleeping on it"
3. Insight—the intuitive "aha!" that appears like a piece of a puzzle you didn't even know you were solving

At the point that you have an insight, the next phase is closing the window *part way* so that you can use your expertise to shape a solution:

4. Evaluation—application of your expertise to figuring out if what seems like a solution really is one
5. Realization—translating your idea into a plan of action and bringing your solution to reality

Because many of our daily tasks are repetitive, when problems arise we tend to skip straight to step four and from there to step five. I'm calling that a *closed* process, because there is no opportunity to challenge basic assumptions; we just decide we're right and move on from there. Of course, it makes sense to apply past learning to many if not most problems; doing so saves time and allows us to achieve specific, predictable goals. However, this is not creative. Being creative means slowing down our decision-making so that we have time to fully explore all of the possibilities before we start evaluating options; it's an *open* process.

Steps one and two—identification and incubation—are kind of like putting all of the ingredients in your refrigerator out on the counter before you decide what you're going to make for dinner, then taking a walk instead of coming to any decisions. As hard as it can be to take the time to let images or thoughts bubble up and incubate, studies have shown that without that investment, step three—insight—is unlikely to happen.

And then, after taking all the time needed to complete steps one to three, step four— evaluation—is tough for a different reason. How heartbreaking it is to evaluate an insight and find we need to go back to the drawing board. Yet solving a tough problem often requires going over and over again through steps two through four until a workable solution is developed.

Lastly, once we are confident that our insight has produced a viable solution, developing it into a plan of action (step five, realization) puts us back into territory most of us are more comfortable with; though as you'll see, even here being creative is important.

Preparing for the Process

It's important to understand that creativity is not truly an orderly, step-by-step process; if you expect a tidy path, you may become discouraged. The only reason we use steps in this guide is that there is a natural flow to starting with the discovery of a challenge and ending up somewhere downstream at a plan for implementing an idea. However, like da Vinci's water flows, your creative process will spend some time swirling around obstacles before it actually gets all the way to an accomplished goal.

In the context of our busy lives, that's hard to take. "Okay, that didn't work out so well; let's go back to the beginning and see if we can make this better" can be frustrating and difficult to accept. Besides, what *really* bothers us is the feeling that we don't know if our efforts are ever going to amount to anything; it's scary.

So before you get started, get your mind in the right place. A worthwhile goal deserves a little bravery. Yes, you might fail, but on the other hand if you succeed you'll have done something pretty heroic. Just start with step one and see where the process takes you. You'll get there!

Step 1: Identification

Exercises on page 29

Identification of a creative challenge begins with perceiving a problem or an opportunity in a new way. You just can't be creative if you perceive the world the same old way, never questioning or being curious about anything. So if you want to be creative, be prepared to actually go *looking* for things that intrigue, puzzle or bother you.

That's not part of the usual routine, so it means breaking old habits and installing new ones. For one person, it may mean slowing down and putting unused senses to work in observing the world. For another, it may mean being more courageous and willing to challenge the status quo.

Challenges that motivate you to become actively creative may involve something that troubles you. You may be motivated to "fix" what seems wrong. On the other hand, your challenge may spring from truly loving a subject or activity; you may be motivated to explore something new. Both impulses can lead you to identify creative challenges.

However you get there, don't stop looking for challenges until you're feeling energized. The key test for whether you've found a challenge that will sustain your creative process is how motivated you are. If the challenge suddenly seems to spring up everywhere you go, or if it floats around in your mind when you should be doing something else, you've found it.

Step 2: Incubation

Exercises on page 32

When you come up with a challenge that's motivating, nurture your curiosity and interest in it. Before grabbing onto a solution, explore everything about it and see if you can make it even more motivating. Let it slosh around in your mind, stepping away from it and back to it as you go through your daily life.

When you do work on your challenge, immerse yourself by asking lots of open-ended, wide-ranging questions. Be particularly curious about the environment surrounding your challenge. Ask what would make this really exciting to me? To others? Explore topics that may seem slightly off the central question, but have strong emotional resonance. The more open and flexible your interest in your challenge, the more rich your exploration will be.

For example, if your challenge is to develop a product for homeowners, investigate their lives and values, not just how they use products:

- What do they do around the house in their free time?
- What's the most important thing to them? What are the next two most important things?
- What are they most concerned about? What are the next two things they are most concerned about?

Don't just read all about it. Observe videos, songs, films, social media; use all of your senses to help you to understand your context. Talk to people you know, talk to strangers for that matter, and ask open ended questions; e.g., "what do you think?" not "do you like my idea?"

Let your thoughts flow freely around what your curiosity is exploring. Go as deep as you can, take notes, and bookmark or save the information rather than edit it. Pull out random notes and re-read them. Sleep on it. Get out of your patterns and habits as far as you are able. Take a different route to work. Turn off the TV, power down the Blackberry. Don't let yourself become passive or allow interruptions to keep your mind from flowing freely.

Your incubation period could be a week, or a year. Doubts will come up: you may feel pressured if someone else is working on the same problem or discouraged because others before you have tried to do this and failed. If it were easy to break new ground, everyone would be doing it. They're not. You may sometimes feel on your own.

On those days, only your commitment will carry you through. Keep positive people around you. If your project is work-based, weed out the naysayers. If it's for your daily life, surround yourself with others who are inspired by you and want to inspire you in turn. Don't look back, don't turn around. Keep moving forward.

INSPIRATION: IF YOU CAN'T SOLVE ONE PROBLEM, SOLVE ANOTHER

Some diseases stubbornly resist the creativity of doctors and scientists. One such disease, rheumatoid arthritis, can be very

hard to treat and manage. Over the long course of this disease, patients become resistant to treatments or develop bad reactions to them. Then the doctor introduces a new drug, starting the cycle all over again. This exhausting search for ways to help patients makes both patient and doctor frustrated and depressed.

Facing up to the reality that even the best drugs don't yet cure this debilitating disease, one of my clients decided to focus on helping patients in other ways. To develop an idea for what we could do, they brought doctors, patients, scientists, and company executives through a series of sessions designed to identify feelings, images, and ideas for what could make things better. They tried many different research approaches, as well as open-ended discussions and brainstorming.

Using empathy as our Identification exercise, we had perceived a need to design a program of lifetime patient support. Our incubation explored ways we could create a program that addressed the whole person, not just the disease. Social life, financial stress, even romance were areas our program could address. We used many group sessions to involve all of the people who are responsible for helping these patients, and we included patients themselves.

Interestingly, some of our best ideas came from scientific, analytic types who had never done anything like this before. The pride in their faces proved that being creative is a reward in itself.

Step 3: Insight

Exercises on page 33

Finding insights can be a confusing process. For one thing, how do you know when you've found one that's really insightful?

Insights are extraordinary moments of clarity that illuminate something that was hidden. When you find one, there will be a feeling of "Oh!" or "Aha!" That may not sound very scientific, but that's the point: insights have an intuitive quality. The feeling of revelation itself is a sign that you've had an insight. It's not necessary that you be the first person to ever discover your insight. It's how it helps you that matters.

From time to time, while you're incubating your challenge, a glimmer of an insight will arise. You'll rush to jot it down, then not be sure why when you read it again. You may want to go back over your incubation notes to be sure you're on track. Feel free to do that, as long as you're mulling it over, not scrapping it (we need to postpone analysis and judgment for step four).

If you have more than one insight, that's not only fine, it's fantastic. It may be that a group of insights work well together. To bring it back to da Vinci:

- He <u>identified</u> his topic of interest by observing the world, perceiving that water forms specific shapes when it flows around rocks, and became curious about that

- He <u>incubated</u> his interest in water, filling notebooks with observations and insights. He observed how vortices formed, how the different levels of force of joined bodies of water shaped their movement.

- Among the hundreds of <u>insights</u> he uncovered about water flows, one was that managing water flows could make mills work better.

When you feel that you have found an insight, use it to clarify your challenge. Insightful challenges are:

- Phrased as simple, one-sentence statements (extraordinary clarity should make your ideas themselves beautifully simple)

- Exciting and different enough to challenge you and use your talents

- Motivating to you, yet inclusive of and even motivating to others as well

Then re-write your challenge, informed by your insight (the exercises for this step will help you with this). For example:

> If the starting problem was: Extend my industrial agriculture company into consumer markets.
>
> The insightful challenge could be: *Make growing your own food a year-round source of family health and fun.*

What a difference! The insightful challenge stems from the original problem, but has deepened into something that might actually motivate both a company and its audience.

The more insightful it is, the more ready your challenge is to be tested in the real world. Because you've taken the time to clearly perceive your challenge and its environment, you're in the best possible position to see if it can actually work.

Take a moment and celebrate your breakthrough, but don't get too comfortable. We still need to turn your insightful challenge into a real, workable, *creative* idea.

INSPIRATION: BEING MOTIVATED TO CREATE

What happens when two young people, deeply in love, have completely different life plans? He wants to be a successful technology entrepreneur in San Francisco; she wants to help poor business people in Africa... You might think their marriage was doomed if they couldn't even agree on a continent. Yet Matt and Jessica Flannery brought their seemingly disparate goals together in a wildly successful, creative idea—Kiva.org, a social network-based microlender. (*Microfinance,* creatively invented by Nobel winner Muhammed Yunus, means providing small loans to poor entrepreneurs who have no other access to capital).

The Flannery's went through all of the steps we've talked about here. Early on in their identification process they agreed that they wanted to sponsor businesses in poor countries, but the insightful challenge that resulted in Kiva.org took a lot of incubation. They talked to many people in many different places and walks of life, and discovered plenty of surprising insights along the way: for example, most Americans who are interested in sponsoring microloans are turned off by for-profit programs.

Still, I believe that the ultimate source of their creativity was their motivation to have a fabulous marriage.

Step 4: Evaluation

Exercises on page 34

At the beginning of this chapter, I said that for step four you close the window of your creativity *part way.* That's because while you are going to evaluate your idea by bringing your expertise and knowledge to assessing its viability, you also need to balance that with a desire to make your idea better, not kill it.

If you (or others around you) approach this step as an up or down vote, creativity is choked off and great ideas will be thrown out for no good reason. Instead, put your idea through a flight simulator, inventing a variety of scenarios, and turning obstacles into new creative questions. Your goal is to make your idea stronger than it would have been otherwise.

For example, take our consumer agriculture product idea from step three. The insightful challenge was: *Make growing your own food a year-round source of family health and fun.* Let's say that the product is hydroponics, and we've decided to create home hydroponics kits. (Hydroponics means growing food in water instead of soil, using some basic lighting and pumping equipment and adding nutrients to the water.)

In the "flight test" for this idea, several potential obstacles arise. One by one, we transform those obstacles into new creative challenges:

- Obstacle 1: many people who would want to grow plants in water instead of soil live in apartments; the weight of the system could be a problem.

    → Creative challenge: can we reduce the weight to provide a good balance of safety and value?

- Obstacle 2: the distribution network for hydroponics supplies is primarily industrial, and isn't set up for service to consumers.

    → Creative challenge: do we adapt our current system or create a new way to supply consumers?

- Obstacle 3: the equipment we make is pretty pricey for consumers.

    → Creative challenge: how can we finance the period while we scale up production so that we have time to bring unit costs down?

As you can see, in step four we apply our existing expertise to identify the obstacles that arise, and our creativity to reframe them as new creative challenges. Each will be fed back into the creative process for solution, and some of them may result in deep changes to your idea.

This process can be painful: for example, what if research tells us that consumers don't find your hydroponics kit fun? The feedback won't always be good. We have to remain confident that pushing ourselves to be creative about making the idea work will only make it better.

Use your expertise to design your flight test. Be thorough. You will need to explore "make or break" issues such as:

- Access to resources, such as time, money, materials, and specialized skills

- Proof of opportunity: who, what, when, where, how your idea will find a receptive audience

- Need for partnership: who must participate for your idea to work?

Be tough enough to really test your idea, but don't tip over into negativity. Do everything you can to find creative solutions to any obstacles. If you get stuck, *go back and get unstuck.*

INSPIRATION: THE IMPORTANCE OF EXPERTISE

Expertise is different from knowledge, because it comes from actual experience. You can get knowledge by reading a book, but expertise only comes from actually doing something. Some people say it takes ten years to become expert at anything!

Expertise and creativity are a dynamic combination. Jazz musicians are a great example of this dynamic. They study and memorize patterns of notes and harmony, developing their technique through endless hours and years of repetition. Once they have it all down, they are able improvise freely: their expertise empowers them to flow through musical ideas without hesitation.

Expertise is important to all creative people. For one thing, it helps you to find more interesting challenges. If you really understand a subject, your perceptions become deeper and more complex. If you are expert enough, you will be able to find the areas of a topic that are still obscure, or discover aspects that need creative solutions. In addition, expertise is a critical tool when you evaluate an idea. Being able to foresee the obstacles facing your idea requires experience as well as imagination.

As you evaluate your idea, be sure to get any help you need from others who are more expert than you are. Don't let their criticism discourage you; use it to help you make your idea stronger.

Step 5: Realization

Exercises on page 35

Realization is the step where you plan how you're going to bring your idea to reality. Your execution plan will typically include:

- The people who need to be involved, with their roles and responsibilities
- Concrete steps that everyone will take to make the idea real
- A list of the support needed, including budgets, tools, and so on

The more you've flight-tested your idea in step four, the clearer your path to actually executing it will be. And yet, you will find new challenges and problems arising all along the path.

That's because if you're breaking new ground, old execution processes may not work. Your creativity will have led you onto paths that are unfamiliar and that require new expertise, which means new discoveries and challenges. Even your execution plan will need to be creative. Designing your execution plan is *yet another creative act*.

This time, let's use as our example a family vacation. You decided that one way to make vacation planning more creative would be to engage your kids in planning with you, and they tell you they want to go to the moon. You took the challenge on, and you've been insightful and creative. You evaluated your options, and designed a camping adventure for your family with astronaut-like tasks in which you will all explore the earth as if it were another planet. You've had so much fun working it all out that you feel like a kid again yourself.

Now it's time to work out your budget and actually plan the trip. And lo and behold the price tag is… astronomical.

Instead of being discouraged, you take your cost problem to step one of the creative process. Once there, you incubate the challenge of how to reduce the cost of your vacation for a few days. You realize that you've been locked into the "long family road trip" mindset of your usual vacations. If you are willing to re-think that, you can design a lower-cost vacation that your kids will love just as much.

If you let it, your motivation will carry you through. Make sure you keep having fun. The more you enjoy being creative, the more you will appreciate that the demand for even more creativity will never end… and that's a great thing.

INSPIRATION: OVERCOMING SELF-LIMITATION

Interestingly, Leonardo da Vinci was not a master at realization. Some of his ideas were probably left on the drawing board because Renaissance technology just wasn't advanced enough, but I also think he may have enjoyed the process of his imagination too much to be truly motivated to execute his ideas. He wanted to move on to the next one. Given how much he did successfully accomplish in his life, we can forgive him.

There are certainly many good ideas which I never acted on. The self-imposed limitations will be familiar: I didn't have enough time, I didn't have the expertise I needed, my idea would cost too much.

With the support and encouragement of those around me, I've managed to turn that around. When I have an idea, I share it with those I trust. Their input and support makes me far more likely to overcome obstacles and stay energized.

Congratulations!

You've motivated yourself, defined an insightful challenge, and found a creative solution.

Take a rest if you need to, but don't let the energy fade.

You've come this far, now see your idea through.

You can do it!

IV. A Quick Guide to Group Brainstorming

Unless you're in a creative profession, such as design or copywriting, the most common creative tool used in a corporate setting is *brainstorming*. Brainstorming was invented in the forties as a way to make the creative process more productive for business purposes.

Brainstorming uses a group to produce many different ideas, as a substitute for enriching the perceptions of individual people. A group of people with different, yet equally expert perspectives imitate what your individual brain might do if you gave it time to explore. Brainstorming therefore proceeds in a more linear way from an open to a closed process, generating many ideas and then using the team's expertise to sort them and shape them into a few useful ideas.

The five steps of brainstorming are very similar to the five steps of the creative process, though far less time is allotted to incubation and insight:

1. **Briefing**. Briefing materials and a purpose statement that expose the challenge to those who will participate. (Typically, a business problem will already have been defined, if not, the briefing may be a separate session that further refines the challenge.)

2. **Exploration**. Together, review examples and illustrative materials that explore and exemplify the challenge. Discuss and capture the raw observations and questions that occur to participants. If necessary answers are not available, postpone the next step until they are found or until the group agrees to set the questions aside.

3. **Ideation**. Group members call out their ideas, all of which are captured without judgment, and "built on" by others who are inspired by them. Require at least one or two "builds" on every idea generated before you move on to the next, forcing group members to listen to one another and

create better ideas. Post the ideas on individual sheets on a board; if some ideas are very similar they can be combined.

4. **Evaluation**. Develop criteria for assessment of the ideas, such as customer needs, business goals, etc. Ask each team member to apply his or her expertise to ensure that all criteria are identified; capture the list and post it. Then discuss each idea and make a list of open issues; do not eliminate any ideas at this stage.

5. **Prioritization**. Based on the evaluation step, each group member picks their top three ideas, in 1 – 2 – 3 order. You can use sticky notes to do this. Any idea that received a high rating from a group member is discussed, with reference back to the original goals of the group. Based on a consensus, a few ideas are selected for further development and presentation to management.

I cannot emphasize strongly enough that brainstorming is a non-hierarchical, group activity. Groups ensure that ideas are balanced across a variety of knowledge-sets; this diversity of perspective can help to keep the energy going long enough to get to a true breakthrough. Work with a minimum of three people with different and complementary areas of expertise, and an absolute maximum of eight. If the group is too small, it will run out of ideas very quickly; if too big, some people won't be heard.

Lastly, for brainstorming to work, mutual respect is critical. If some people are not contributing, make everyone take turns. Be flexible about group composition; for example, if necessary, isolate domineering members by pulling them into a small group all their own. If you are facilitating a brainstorming that includes the boss, and you notice that people are too deferential, nicely ask her or him to find something else to do for a while. I have seen many companies fail at coming up with ideas because of a very human tendency to flatter those in power.

Exercises and Comments

- Summary of the Active Creative Process
- Step One: Identification Exercises
- Step Two: Incubation Exercises
- Step Three: Insight Exercises
- Step Four: Evaluation Exercises
- Step Five: Realization Exercises
- When Do You *Have* to Be Creative?
- The Commitment

Summary of the Active Creative Process

Opening the window of creativity:

1. Identification—immersing yourself in something that makes you curious; feeling interest until you identify a motivating challenge

    - Observe without judgment, become curious, and truly perceive the world around you.

2. Incubation—letting ideas develop over time; exploring all the topic openly and freely; "sleeping on it"

    - Trust your unconscious mind; don't judge or censor your thoughts. Continue to observe and be curious.

3. Insight—the "aha!" that appears like a piece of a puzzle you didn't even know you were solving

    - Find the "aha!" that turns your original problem into an insightful challenge that really motivates you.

Closing the window *part way* so that you can use your expertise:

4. Evaluation—application of your expertise to figuring out if what seems like a solution really is one

    - Conduct a flight test that identifies obstacles and turn each obstacle into a new creative challenge. Be prepared to change your idea as needed to make it achievable.

5. Realization—translating your idea into a plan of action and bringing your solution to reality

    - Avoid fatigue by reconfirming your commitment. Be creative about how you execute your idea.

Step 1: Identification Exercises

Identifying a creative challenge is in many ways the most important step in the creative process. Persistent creators like da Vinci find this easy, but most people need to set aside time and effort to get started.

In working with corporate clients and on my own projects, I have identified some exercises that are helpful, and I'm outlining them here. Different personalities may find some of these approaches more comfortable than others; I encourage you to consider trying at least one that's *not* an easy fit for you.

1. *Reach for the stars.* If you are the top at something, how could you do even better? What would that mean... changing half the ingredients in your signature dish? redefining your industry? If you're at the bottom, could you get to the top within X years? Make a list of all of your ideas, and keep doing that until there isn't one idea left in you. Do not be realistic. Do not be practical. Be outrageous.

   Observe without judging: what do you keep scratching off your list, and why the heck are you doing that?
   Be curious: what do you see that no-one else sees?

   Examples of a challenge:

   - *Our company could be five times our size.* Transform my industrial company into a consumer company.

   - *I think I've grown really expert; now I'd like to share what I know.* Take my knitting skills out into the world, perhaps as a knitting teacher.

2. *Use your envy.* Deadly sin or not, envy is your friend when it tells you what you want. Who or what out there do you envy? What about a celebrity or a master chef? What about your girlfriend's smug old cat? Figure out what it is that arouses envy in you and then get obsessed with it. What are the qualities that make it so great at something? Make a list of the qualities you'd like to emulate, and make getting there your problem.

   Observe without judging: how did the object of your envy end up in such a prized position?

Be curious: what or who else do you envy, and how does it all connect?

Examples of a challenge:

- *I wish I were like Sully Sullenberger, the pilot who landed in the Hudson River.* Make my local construction company into a calm and capable hero to our customers.

- *I wish I were like my neighbor Sam.* Be the kind of person who wakes up every morning with a smile on their face.

3. *Empathize 'til it hurts*. We often expect others around us to put up with our quirks and faults. But what if the frustration others experience in their daily lives were painful to us? Spend some time watching people living with a problem (especially if that problem is you or your company). Listen—really listen—to their boredom, disappointment, fear, or anger.

With that in your heart, make a list of all of the things you would change if you had absolute power to make it happen. Changing attitudes is hard—that's why looking at what's wrong with our own attitude is a *great* place to find a challenge.

Observe without judging: what is behind the negative emotions of other people?

Be curious: if they were in your place, what would they do differently?

Examples of a challenge:

- *I want to enjoy my job more, but my customers are so cranky.* Help my store's customers to enjoy their day.

- *My son struts but underneath it all he's scared.* Join with my son in making him confident in school.

4. *Overthrow your hierarchies*. Hierarchies are specifically designed to move challenges out of our space and into someone else's. When someone's clearly in charge, those around him or her fall into lock-step. Well, marching around in formation is no way to stimulate creativity.

If you want new ideas to come out of a group of people, you probably need to shake things up, by putting a junior team member in charge of idea generation, for example, or letting your kids help you plan the family vacation. Let them make the list! Don't censor it, laugh at it, or fear it—learn from it.

Observe without judging: how different skills and traits approach problems in different ways.

Be curious: about how mixing and matching those qualities might lead to a different definition of the problem, let alone a solution.

Examples of a challenge:

- *It turns out that our quality problems start with bad communication.* Help every member of our team be heard and respected.

- *The kids want to go to the moon on vacation.* Design a vacation that makes them feel like they're astronauts exploring another planet.

Step 2: Incubation Exercises

Incubation is a process of feeding and deepening your curiosity about your challenge. Momentum should build along with your interest in your idea. You can be very professional about it and conduct interviews or structured research, or you can be more intuitive and engage in a sort of scrapbooking process of searching, clipping, bookmarking, reading, and so on. Either way, you should amass observations and potential insights, with little or no censorship as to what is relevant. If it feels relevant, keep it on hand. You can always discard it later.

If you don't trust yourself to persist, set a schedule. Set checkpoints. Every Saturday afternoon, or more often if you're on a roll, go through your notes and take notes on the notes. What pops out? Is anything surprising? What is clearer than it was? What is less clear? What's next?

Here's a suggested list of incubation exercises:

- Extend your exploration to related topics. For example, if you are interested in developing a resource for knitters, see what works and doesn't work for scrapbookers.

- Be childish. Play around with your notes by mixing and matching them randomly. Make up a little tune for your idea, or draw a cartoon. Role-play a critic and a supporter. Giggle. (Yeah, you.)

- Create an inner world for your idea. For example, if you want to start a business, visit lots of different small businesses and soak up their energy and environments. Use that detail to make your ideas more real to you.

- Stop checking your e-mail all the time. Interruption is the enemy; once interrupted, you will lose track of your ideas.

- Smile while you are working. Smiling helps you take pleasure in what you are doing, and enjoying yourself is critical to creativity.

Step 3: Insight Exercises

Developing an insight into an "insightful challenge statement" is a challenge in itself. I call these statements *haiku*, after the Japanese poetry form that distills something essential into a very few syllables. Your insightful challenge statement should tease out the single most motivating challenge and most revealing insight.

Fill out this table, using the minimum words necessary:

Your challenge	Your insight	Your motivation
There can only be one; if you have two or more, choose the one that is most motivating to you.	Roll your key insights into to a primary insight. Keep it simple. Imagine yourself answering a child's question, "why?"	Your motivation may have deepened or changed as you incubated your idea. Take the time to express it very clearly.

Once you've filled out these three columns, it's a lot easier to simplify and clarify your insightful challenge. For example, Impressionist painter Vincent Van Gogh might have completed this chart as follows:

His challenge	His insight	His motivation
Create new kinds of three dimensional effects	The way art is taught is so limiting that it shuts down our ability to accurately perceive the world	Share my excitement about what it means to perceive the reality of light, color and shadow

Based on this chart, his insightful challenge could be: Find new ways to create three dimensional effects that open the windows of perception for painters and their audiences.

Step 4: Evaluation Exercises

A positive critique of your idea has to look at it from every possible angle. Make a detailed list of everything that has to be resolved for your idea to work; this chart suggests some broad topics.

Business issues	Personal issues	Artistic issues
Costs	Affordability	Originality
Skills required	Support needs	Materials needed
Equipment/resources	Family/friend responses	Skills required
Competition	Time needed	Grant availability
Marketing issues	Etc.	Etc.
Etc.		

Each obstacle should be faced squarely, but should be treated as a creative challenge to be solved. Apply the three pillars of active creativity:

- Intention: continue to seek creative solutions to all obstacles that come between you and your intention to create; if that involves re-examining your original idea to make it better, do so
- Perception: if you are blocked, look farther and deeper. Get perspective from someone who isn't so close to the problem; are you sure you have really understood what's possible?
- Play: stay light-hearted and energized; use your imagination to run "what if" scenarios about issues which come up.

Stage four is a great time to tap into the expertise of other people to overcome challenges you don't know how to solve. Reframe your obstacles as creative challenges, and bring them to people who have solved challenges like this before. You may find that what seemed insurmountable to you has been solved many times in the past.

Step 5: Realization Exercises

If you have done a great job in all the other steps, yet find yourself stuck when it comes to creating a detailed plan to achieve your goal, you need some self-diagnosis.

As your process converges on reality, it's pretty common to be frozen in a "deer in the headlights" fear of bringing your idea to reality. This could spring from a couple of sources:

- Do you find yourself eager to focus on some new idea before you bring the old one to completion? You may be addicted to the open part of the process—where you feel brilliant without ever being tested.

 I need to be a little stern with you. In our fantasy lives, everyone is a ballet star, a rock and roll legend, a great leader. But only in the real world can you truly become one. Risking failure takes courage; be a hero!

- Do you find the time required and financial costs too risky? That's legitimate, but it's not a reason to completely quit. Ask yourself two questions:

  o Can I scale this back so it's more achievable? Even large companies run trials before they jump in with both feet.

  o What help is available to me? Micro-loans, grants, venture capital, the small business administration, and local chambers of commerce may be able to help you work out your difficulties.

 Remain committed, and be creative about fitting your project into your life. Don't take foolish risks that could hurt yourself or others, but don't freeze up at all thought of risk. Get help to find a middle ground where you feel in control.

Here's a quick list of other obstacles to watch out for in step five, and indeed all along your creative path:

Ego. Egotism shuts down creativity when it strives to protect pride or dominate others. In ourselves, ego can make us unwilling to admit we're wrong or take necessary risks. In groups, a single selfish or arrogant person can bully or humiliate others enough to shut down a creative process. If this happens, address it. The goal matters, not anyone's ego.

Fatigue. Creative processes take significant work. No matter how committed you are, a day will come when you decide you just can't do this anymore. Realize is that this is just one day. Clear your mind, remember your motivation, and reach out to your support network, committing yourself to come back to your challenge with fresh eyes and a renewed spirit.

Fear. Fear is natural, but if you don't rise above it and embrace the fun of invention, your brain won't be creative. If you find you are afraid, try to understand why. Do you lack the support you need? Then go out and get it. Are you just worried that you will fail? Face your fear, name it, and find a solution.

The Grind. Creativity takes work, but most of the time it should *feel* more like play. If you find creativity to be a grind, you may unwittingly have shut your creative process down. I suggest that you surround yourself with music, art, toys, any anything else that inspires the playful side of your personality. And remember to smile!

Time. It's hard to find the time to be creative. Maybe you need to bring a notebook or your PDA with you wherever you go, so you can jot down ideas. It will help if people you spend time with are also engaged in your challenge. And you have to make time tradeoffs, making space for creativity in your schedule.

When Do You *Have* to Be Creative?

When to engage in a creative process can be an important decision. At a minimum, we have to recognize situations when we absolutely need to get our talent for creativity out of the attic and dust it off, because established habits and patterns aren't going to do the trick.

We may identify a need for creativity when we encounter an obstacle in our field of expertise, for example. After throwing everything we've got at it for months or years, we may realize that what is already known isn't going to solve this challenge. If we had identified the need for creative thinking earlier, we might have saved ourselves from frustration and unproductive work. Ideally, we can learn to spot the kinds of challenges that demand creative solutions before we've wasted too much time.

The table below shows examples of typical situations in which we find ourselves to be *stuck*. "Stuckness" is a varied experience; it can be frustrating, worrying, or even just boring. The worst situation is one in which no-one realizes they are stuck. Bad relationships and ongoing international conflicts are an example of this. It's as if, every day, the people who are stuck wake up, repeat the same reactions, and go to bed without having learned anything.

Honing your impatience with stuckness is a great way to become an active creator. Self-defeating patterns *should* drive you crazy. Another cure for stuckness is curiosity. Curiosity will help you to challenge the ideas that got you stuck in the first place. If people believe the world is flat, they won't take the risk of sailing off into the distance far enough to realize it's actually round! But if they're curious enough, they may want to see what the ends of the earth really look like.

You can use the following table to see if there are any stuck areas in your life or work that might require creative solutions.

Situations that demand creativity	Two examples from daily life:	Two examples from business:
You find yourself "solving" the same problem again and again and again and…	• Recurring fights with a spouse or child • Recurring budget problems	• Inability to break through a business problem • Persistent drain of talent from your company
Change is forced on you unexpectedly and you're filled with self-doubt	• Job loss • Relationship loss	• Strong new competitor • Loss of your biggest customer
An opportunity comes in your door that (even if it's positive) makes you feel inexpert and uncomfortable	• You receive a windfall and have to learn to manage money • Child uncovers a talent that demands time and money	• An opportunity arises and you're not sure you can handle it • There's a new technology that could be huge, or not
You're worried by a negative trend	• Someone in your life is out of sorts, and won't discuss it • Your town's services aren't functioning as well as they used to	• Sales trends have changed for no reason you can see • A small competitor is innovating faster than your company

The Commitment

Right here, right now, say to yourself:

I am going to follow this where it leads me.

The path may be broken in places, but I will be persistent.

...I'm worth it.
...My family is worth it.
...My company is worth it.
...My customers are worth it.
...The world is worth it.

Are you there?

Now you are prepared to be creative.

Notes

Page 1. Mallett, Ronald (2006). *Time Traveler: A Scientist's Personal Mission to Make Time Travel a Reality.* Thunder's Mouth Press.

Page 3. Alexander Fleming. (2011, March 6). In *Wikipedia, The Free Encyclopedia.* Retrieved 18:40, March 7, 2011.
http://en.wikipedia.org/w/index.php?title=Alexander_Fleming&oldid=417410311

Page 4. Leonardo da Vinci. (2011, February 20). In *Wikipedia, The Free Encyclopedia.*
http://en.wikipedia.org/w/index.php?title=Leonardo_da_Vinci&oldid=414912117

Page 6. Creativity. (2011, February 16). In *Wikipedia, The Free Encyclopedia.*
http://en.wikipedia.org/w/index.php?title=Creativity&oldid=414296378

Page 7. Flaherty, A. W. (2005). "Frontotemporal and dopaminergic control of idea generation and creative drive". *Journal of Comparative Neurology* 493 (1): 147–153.

Page 7. Allen, John S., PhD. Creativity, the Brain, and Evolution: Creativity: Adaptation or a byproduct of increased intelligence? *Psychology Today.* Published on April 29, 2010.

Page 10. "They All Laughed", 1937. Music George Gershwin with lyrics by Ira Gershwin.

Page 14. Cziksentmihalyi, Mihaly. *Creativity: Flow and the Psychology of Discovery and Invention* (1996), published by HarperCollins e-books.

Page 20. Flannery, Matt. "Kiva and the Birth of Person-to-Person Microfinance." (2007) *Innovations: Winter and Spring 2007.* MIT Press.

About the Author

My own interest in creativity spans all areas of my life: creative writing, marketing strategy, being a daughter, sister, wife and mother, even being a citizen. Over the years I have also been inspired by watching others re-invent their lives when things went wrong, or start successful businesses, or create beautiful music.

Arising from all this inspiration, a few years ago I founded The Market Artist. The Market Artist is a consultancy dedicated to inspiring creativity in marketing strategy. With thirty years' experience across a wide variety of disciplines, industries and target markets, I've distilled an approach to creating marketing ideas that are human, simple, and strong.

This book is my attempt to share some of what I've learned with you, in the hope that creativity will enrich not just your business but your life. Let me know if I succeeded!

E-mail me at victoria@activelycreative.com.

www.ingramcontent.com/pod-product-compliance
Lightning Source LLC
Chambersburg PA
CBHW051719040426
42446CB00008B/960